DEVELOPING EMOTIONAL INTELLIGENCE IN KIDS

A Guide to Understanding and Developing EI In Kids

Melissa Smith White

Copyright © 2023, Melissa Smith White
All rights reserved.

No part of this book may be reproduced or transmitted in any form or by any means, electronic or mechanical, including photocopying, recording, or any information storage or retrieval system, without written permission from the author.

Table of Contents

Developing Emotional Intelligence In Kids

Introduction

Emotional intelligence has developed as an essential skill set for people of all ages, including children, given the fast-paced and connected world we live in. We value developing not just our children's academic success but also their emotional health and social skills as parents, educators, and caregivers.

"Emotional Intelligence for Kids" takes readers on and explores emotional intelligence's transforming potential and its significant effects on kids' lives. This subject aims to equip parents, educators, and anyone else engaged in the development of children to recognize and develop emotional intelligence as a crucial life skill.

The capacity to comprehend, control, and regulate one's own emotions, as well as to sympathize with and successfully interact with others, is referred to as emotional intelligence. It is essential to help kids overcome obstacles, form positive connections, and develop resilience in the face of life's ups and downs.

We will examine several facets of emotional intelligence in this investigation, offering perceptions and useful tips for fostering emotional intelligence in kids of all ages. "Emotional Intelligence for Kids" will provide you with the skills to empower kids in their emotional development and social growth, from understanding and expressing emotions to handling stress and conflict.

Join us on this trip as we learn how emotional intelligence may have a transforming impact on children's emotional health, academic achievement, and general happiness. Together, let's cultivate an atmosphere that is encouraging and nurturing emotional intelligence, giving the next generation the fundamental abilities they need to succeed in a world that is always changing.

Developing Emotional Intelligence In Kids

Chapter One

Understanding Emotional Intelligence In Kids

The capacity to successfully identify, comprehend, and control one's own emotions as well as the emotions of others is known as emotional intelligence (EI). It entails being conscious of one's feelings, utilizing those feelings to shape one's decisions and actions, and interacting with others with empathy and compassion. EI is important for both personal and social well-being because it affects how people see and express themselves, build and sustain relationships, and deal with difficulties.

Alex and Emma are two siblings with distinct ways of processing their emotions, to explain the idea of emotional intelligence. They had comparable struggles with peers and in school.

They reacted to these circumstances emotionally in different ways. However, the oldest brother, Alex, would become hostile and protective if he ran across problems or got feedback from peers or professors. He struggled to manage his emotions and behaviors, so he would snap at others. Alex often responded to questions about his thoughts with annoyance, refusing to go further into the causes of such feelings.

Emma, the younger sister, on the other hand, handled her issues differently. She would stop when confronted with a similar circumstance and consider how she felt. She was aware of her feelings and knew it was OK to be angry or dissatisfied. Emma would subsequently approach her instructor or friend and respectfully explain her ideas and emotions.

Over time, Alex's emotional outbursts caused his relationships with instructors and classmates to become strained. He was even more enraged and frustrated because he felt alone and misunderstood. Emma, on the other hand, developed deep and significant relationships with others. Her professors and friends loved her because she was empathetic and had good communication skills.

At their school, my team and I exclusively talked about emotional intelligence. The goal of the program was to educate students about emotional intelligence and help them develop it.

Emma enthusiastically engaged in the class, sharing her experiences and demonstrating a willingness to learn more about emotions and their effects. Alex first resisted because he felt awkward exploring his feelings. But as the session went on, he began to understand the value of emotional intelligence and how it may enhance his interpersonal interactions and general well-being.

The students were provided with numerous methods and tools for boosting emotional intelligence, including active listening, mindfulness activities, and empathy training. Self-awareness, empathy, and effective communication were promoted via these exercises.

Emma continued to use these emotional intelligence techniques over the next weeks and saw improvements in her interactions and relationships. She felt more capable of addressing disagreements and more prepared to comprehend others' viewpoints.

Inspired by his sister's development, Alex decided to try out emotional intelligence. He started meditating and reflecting, which helped him gradually acquire control over his emotions. He saw that others reacted to him more favorably as he learned to express his emotions healthily, and he had a stronger sense of connection with others.

Both Alex and Emma kept honing their emotional intelligence over time. As siblings, they became closer to one another and supported one another's development and self-awareness.

Emotional intelligence is crucial in determining how people react to difficulties and interact with others. It enables individuals to communicate successfully, comprehend their feelings, and sympathize with others. People like Alex and Emma may lead more rewarding lives, cultivate meaningful relationships, and successfully navigate the ups and downs of life by increasing their emotional intelligence.

Chapter Two

Why Emotional Intelligence Matters for Kids

Children's emotional intelligence (EI) is very important since it forms the basis for their whole social, emotional, and emotional health. Their capacity to comprehend and control their own emotions, sympathize with others, form deep connections with others, and successfully deal with life's obstacles is significantly shaped by this. Let's examine in further detail why emotional intelligence is important for children and the many advantages it offers to their lives:

Children who possess emotional intelligence are better able to identify and comprehend their feelings. Kids who are conscious of their emotions are better able to express themselves and articulate their needs, which strengthens their sense of self and boosts their self-confidence.

Emotionally intelligent children have greater emotional control. They develop effective coping mechanisms for dealing with intense emotions like anger, frustration, or grief, which lessens impulsive actions and outbursts. They can respond resolutely to pressure and disappointments thanks to their emotional self-control.

Emotional intelligence helps children develop empathy and compassion. Children grow more sensitive to other people's sentiments as they recognize and comprehend their own emotions. Their capacity for empathy improves their interpersonal interactions, encouraging compassion and creating a tolerant and encouraging atmosphere.

Emotionally intelligent children are better at successfully expressing their ideas and emotions. They learn how to actively listen and become better at deciphering nonverbal clues, which enables them to communicate with classmates, instructors, and family members in a clearer and more meaningful way.

Emotional intelligence plays a crucial role in creating and sustaining meaningful relationships. Strong and enduring friendships are more likely to develop among children who can sympathize with others and control their emotions. They foster an environment of trust and understanding, which increases their likeability and approachability.

Emotionally intelligent children are better equipped to manage disagreements healthily. They possess the ability to assertively communicate, actively hear the opinions of others, and identify win-win compromises. These abilities are crucial for creating harmony in the workplace and peaceful dispute resolution.

Academic achievement is favorably impacted by emotional intelligence. Children with great emotional intelligence (EI) are better able to concentrate, manage their time wisely, and cope with the demands of school. When presented with academic problems, they are more persistent and resilient, and more driven to study.

A child's emotional well-being is greatly influenced by their emotional intelligence. Children that have high EI have reduced levels of stress, anxiety, and sadness. They are better able to handle emotional turmoil and have an optimistic attitude toward life.

Children with emotional intelligence are more likely to succeed in the long run in a variety of areas of life. As kids become older, they are more likely to develop into emotionally sophisticated people who have the necessary life skills for both intimate and professional interactions.

Emotionally intelligent children are more likely to develop into good leaders and team members. They are better collaborators and inspirational leaders who can inspire and encourage their colleagues because they are aware of the needs and feelings of others.

Emotional intelligence is crucial for children since it has a significant influence on their social, emotional, and cognitive growth. Children who are raised with emotional intelligence are better equipped to deal with obstacles in life, make meaningful relationships, and succeed in a variety of areas. Fostering emotional intelligence in children is a substantial investment in their future success and well-being as parents, educators, and caregivers.

Chapter Three

Understanding Emotions In Kids

Understanding children's emotions is essential to their emotional growth and general well-being. Children's emotions have a significant impact on their life, influencing their ideas, actions, and relationships with others. Helping children understand and manage their emotions is crucial for fostering emotional intelligence and laying a solid basis for their social and emotional development as parents, carers, and educators.

To comprehend children's emotions, it's important to take into account the following:

Understanding Different Emotions

A child's variety of emotions includes joy, sorrow, rage, fear, enthusiasm, and more. It is crucial to support them in appropriately identifying and naming these feelings. Kids who have this knowledge are better equipped to comprehend their emotions and express them in appropriate ways.

Encourage Emotional Expression

It's important to provide a secure and encouraging atmosphere for children to express their feelings. Encourage honest dialogue and reassure them that it's alright to experience a variety of emotions by validating their sentiments.

Children should be taught that emotions are a normal and valid aspect of being a person. It is common to feel a variety of emotions in reaction to varied circumstances, and every feeling is legitimate and worthy of recognition.

Empathy & Perspective-Taking

Show children how to sympathize with others by taking into account their thoughts and emotions. This capacity for empathy encourages compassion and understanding in their interpersonal interactions.

Help youngsters recognize the bodily and verbal signs that are connected to various emotions. For instance, a raised eyebrow may be an indication of rage, whilst a wide grin may be a reflection of joy. Emotional awareness is improved by recognizing these indicators in oneself and others.

Discuss the circumstances that set off certain emotions, and look at effective coping mechanisms. Teaching children healthy coping mechanisms for their emotions, such as deep breathing or talking to a trusted adult, gives them the capacity to do so.

Emotional Expression Modeling

Children often pick up knowledge by watching adults. Setting a good example for children by talking about their emotions or taking pauses when unhappy, for example, demonstrates healthy emotional expression and management.

Children should be taught that emotions are mutable and that they may change over time. Emphasize that emotions are fleeting and will pass while validating their reactions in various circumstances.

Encourage youngsters to use a wide range of words related to emotions so they may express their emotions clearly. With this terminology, they may communicate their needs for assistance more clearly and succinctly.

Be mindful of how gender and culture might affect how people express their emotions. Insist that there are no "right" or "wrong" feelings and that each person's emotional experiences are distinct and legitimate.

The process of comprehending a child's feelings involves persistence, attentive listening, and sincere support. Children may have a better awareness of themselves and others by being raised in a supportive atmosphere that promotes emotional intelligence, which will result in more positive emotional development and more fulfilling interactions throughout their life.

Developing Emotional Intelligence In Kids

Chapter Four

Managing Emotions

Helping children learn to manage their emotions is a fundamental aspect of their emotional development and personal growth. As kids navigate through various experiences and challenges, understanding and regulating their emotions become essential life skills. By equipping them with effective coping strategies and emotional resilience, we empower kids to face life's ups and downs with confidence and grace. In this section, we will explore the significance of managing emotions in kids and provide valuable insights and techniques for parents, caregivers, and educators to support children in this critical aspect of their emotional intelligence.

I remember vividly when my daughter had a phobia of heights, and all I said to her was "You can do it, baby," "You can control these emotions." It took her some time to reassure herself that she can climb high places by controlling how she feels at that moment. Managing emotions in kids takes a lot of nurturing and patience.

Coping Strategies for Dealing with Negative Emotions

Negative emotional responses are unpleasant and disturbing. Sadness, anxiety, rage, and jealousy are a few examples of unpleasant emotions. Not only are these emotions unpleasant, but they also make it difficult to operate in day-to-day activities and get things done.

It's crucial to remember that no feeling, even an unpleasant one, is intrinsically harmful. Feeling these feelings in certain settings or circumstances is very natural. When these feelings continue and interfere with your child's ability to go about his/her daily activities, they become troublesome.

Fortunately, there are healthier approaches to handling challenging feelings. These coping mechanisms may assist you and your child while also enhancing their capacity to control their emotions.

Recognize Your Kids Feelings
Identify the circumstances in their life that are causing tension and unpleasant feelings by looking inside. It might be helpful to examine the cause of the emotion and how they responded.

A stressful workload is one example of an occurrence that might create negative feelings, and their reflections about a situation can have an impact. Their perspective on what transpired might affect how they feel about it and whether or not it produces tension.

Change What You Can

Until you have a good knowledge and understanding of your child's emotional issues and what triggers them, that is when you can address them critically. They could experience unpleasant feelings less often if they reduce or eliminate some stress triggers.

You might do this in a variety of ways, including:

- Seeking assistance
- Learning aggressive communication techniques
- Changing negative thinking patterns with the cognitive restructuring technique

Regular exercise may uplift your mood and provide you with a way to let out your bad feelings.

Locating possibilities for amusement and increasing humor with your children.

Keep in mind that each person has unique demands and capacities. To discover a strategy that works for you and your child's condition, it's important to often test a few different ones. When your children have the right strategies, they'll feel less overpowered when those unpleasant feelings come up.

Even if your children have a generally optimistic viewpoint, bad feelings will still happen. Learning how to help them manage their emotions now, will help you as parents feel better now and in the future.

Developing Emotional Intelligence In Kids

Chapter Five

Emotional Intelligence at School

My daughter's school organizes what they termed "Emotional Intelligence Day." Where the whole class would participate in activities and discussions that would help them understand and practice emotional intelligence.

The day began with a circle of trust, where students took turns sharing an emotion they had experienced recently. Some spoke of happiness from a recent achievement, while others mentioned feeling nervous before a class presentation. The teachers made sure to emphasize that all emotions were valid and that the class was a safe space to express themselves.

The students also engage in art projects. Each student is given a blank canvas and an array of colorful paints. They were instructed to create an abstract representation of their emotions, allowing their feelings to guide their brushstrokes.

This canvas became a visual reflection of their inner emotions, and they ended up appreciating the power of creative expression in understanding and processing their feelings.

These activities help kids express their thoughts and practice emotional intelligence daily. It enables them to become more empathetic and compassionate, fostering an inclusive and harmonious school environment.

Integrating emotional intelligence (EI), as a crucial component of children's development, into the classroom setting may have a positive impact on student's academic achievement, social relationships, and general well-being. By promoting a supportive and emotionally intelligent learning environment, schools play a crucial role in developing emotional intelligence in kids. Let's go further into the ways that schools may foster students' emotional intelligence:

Emotional Literacy Curriculum

Enhancing students' emotional intelligence may be done effectively by including emotional literacy in the curriculum. Schools may provide classes or activities to help kids identify, categorize, and comprehend their emotions. Discussions, role-playing, or artistic endeavors that promote emotional expression may be included in these classes.

Practices for Cultivating Emotional Awareness
Introducing routines that foster emotional awareness may assist pupils in being more sensitive to their emotions. Children who practice mindfulness techniques, such as deep breathing or guided meditation, may learn to be present and reflect on their feelings without passing judgment.

Techniques for Emotional Regulation It's crucial to provide kids with tools for good emotional management. Schools may instruct students in a variety of coping skills to assist them manage their emotions in stressful circumstances, such as counting to ten, taking a break, or journaling.

Programs for Social and Emotional Learning (SEL)
Adopting SEL practices that are supported by research may greatly improve children's

emotional intelligence. These programs often place a strong emphasis on fostering empathy, social skills, and conflict resolution competencies. SEL may be included in group discussions, classroom activities, and school-wide projects.

Conducting emotional intelligence tests may provide important information about a student's emotional skills and areas for improvement. Teachers may then modify their advice and assistance to accommodate students' unique emotional requirements.

Teachers themselves are essential role models for emotional intelligence when it comes to teaching. The emotional growth of pupils is influenced favorably by instructors who exhibit empathy, active listening, and emotional control.

Emotionally Supportive Atmosphere

Fostering emotional intelligence in schools requires the development of a secure and caring atmosphere. Schools may provide systems of support where kids can express their feelings and get advice, including counseling programs or peer support groups.

Peer mediation programs may be implemented in schools to assist students in helping one another to settle problems amicably. A culture of empathy and understanding is promoted by teaching kids how to communicate effectively and comprehend other people's points of view.

Academic Achievement and Emotional Intelligence

Stressing emotional intelligence has a good effect on academic achievement. Emotionally intelligent students often have greater attention spans, concentration levels, and problem-solving skills, which enhances their academic performance.

Collaboration between parents and schools increases support for children's emotional development by including parents in emotional intelligence efforts. To teach parents how to promote emotional intelligence at home, schools might arrange seminars or family gatherings.

Children's emotional development, resilience, and general well-being are supported by educators by placing a high priority on emotional intelligence in the classroom. Children who have a high level of emotional intelligence are better able to manage stress, have healthy relationships, and excel in school, putting them on the road to a more rewarding and fruitful future.

Developing Emotional Intelligence In Kids

Chapter Six

Emotional Intelligence at Home

Raising compassionate, sympathetic, and emotionally intelligent children is one of our priorities as parents. People that possess emotional intelligence can interact with people, establish connections, and feel connected to them. These folks have the potential to influence others for the better. As parents, we're always looking for new strategies to help kids develop their empathy skills and emotional quotient.

A caring and supportive home environment is built on emotional intelligence. It entails properly identifying, comprehending, and controlling emotions for every family member. The development of emotional intelligence within the context of the family not only improves the well-being of the person but also solidifies family ties and promotes positive interactions. Let's go into the significance of emotional intelligence at home and strategies for fostering it:

Emotional Awareness and Expression

It's important to promote emotional awareness and honest emotional expression at home. Family members need to feel free to express their feelings without fear of condemnation or censure. Family members may foster trust and establish a secure environment for emotional vulnerability by affirming one another's sentiments.

Empathy and Active Listening

The development of emotional intelligence is facilitated by practicing empathy and active listening. Family members' emotional ties are strengthened and disagreements may be addressed more successfully when they sincerely listen to one another and comprehend each other's viewpoints.

Modeling Emotional Intelligence

Parents and other adults who look after children may help youngsters learn how to be emotionally intelligent. Children learn through imitation and are more likely to acquire these abilities themselves when adults exhibit self-awareness, emotional control, and empathy.

Dispute Resolution and Communication

Encourage constructive family communication and dispute resolution. Teach family members to listen to others' perspectives, healthily communicate their wants and feelings, and seek compromises. This makes it possible for family members to settle disputes courteously and sympathetically.

Encourage emotional development in all members of the family by highlighting their accomplishments. Emotional intelligence is reinforced as a worthwhile and desirable attribute when attempts to control emotions are favorably and maturely acknowledged.

Fostering an atmosphere of thankfulness and positive emotions inside the family is important. The emotional climate may be improved and family ties strengthened by expressing thanks to one another and concentrating on pleasant feelings.

Promoting Self-Care

Encourage everyone in the family to practice self-care. Stress the value of taking care of one's emotional health by partaking in activities that foster emotional balance and relaxation.

Empowering Children's Emotional Intelligence

Make emotional intelligence exciting and interesting for kids by including them in projects like art projects, storytelling, or games that are focused on emotions. To foster empathy and emotional awareness, help children recognize their own emotions and those of others.

Setting limits

Setting healthy limits within the family enables members to respect one another's privacy and emotional needs. Having clear boundaries promotes emotional security and guarantees that everyone's emotions are respected.

Teach your family members the value of apologizing and showing forgiveness when disputes happen. Relationships are boosted and emotional healing is encouraged when people can admit wrongdoing and forgive one another.

Practice Recognizing Emotions

We all need social and emotional abilities to function in society, connect with others, and form connections that last a lifetime. As a mother of two young children, I think it's critical to educate kids on how to recognize, express, and healthily regulate their emotions. However, one must first be able to recognize emotions to express and control those feelings.

- Create them
- Play them out.
- Create an emotion or feeling chart.
- Let them ponder

Family members may manage the obstacles of life with resiliency and empathy when there is an emotional intelligence foundation in place at home. Every family member benefits from increased emotional intelligence because they are better able to control their emotions, communicate clearly, and form happier, more meaningful relationships with one another. In the end, encouraging emotional intelligence at home strengthens the family's emotional foundation and improves the well-being and happiness of all its members.

Developing Emotional Intelligence In Kids

Chapter Seven

Emotional Intelligence and Resilience

One of the most crucial qualities somebody can possess is emotional resilience. It is the main characteristic that individuals who live to be over a century old have.

The ability to navigate one's emotions with power and presence while avoiding being overcome by them is known as emotional resilience. By doing this, one may learn from the wisdom and beauty that emotions provide to the human experience and continue to make wise decisions even in the face of strong emotions. Emotional resilience, which is strongly related to emotional intelligence, enables one to recover from challenging circumstances and maybe become stronger than before. By understanding the function of emotional expression and what we can do when our children feel strong emotions, we may encourage this in them.

Emotional Expression's Function

We transport pain through and out of our bodies and minds via emotional expressions, such as sobbing. It is essential to avoid holding onto emotions, whether consciously or unconsciously since this might result in bodily and mental sickness.

Children have strong emotions because they have never experienced pain, disappointment, failure, frustration, or unfavorable situations. For a youngster, each of these common roadblocks is a chance to develop emotional intelligence and resilience.

Failure, struggle, and strong emotions must be normalized if we want children to be emotionally sound. A person with emotional resilience experiences each feeling fully, expresses it in some manner, and then lets it go. Children may proceed through this process through weeping, and efforts to stop them from crying can result in unprocessed experiences and feelings as well as unintended outcomes. Children will eventually naturally transition to other kinds of expression, including talking or being creative.

Parents may guide their kids toward emotional maturity and resilience by teaching them how to accept, be present with, and grow strong in the face of these common components of the human experience. To assist our children cope with emotions with resilience, we must work to prevent them from developing defensive mechanisms like denial, repression, inhibition, mania, victimization, controlling behaviors, or dominance. These mostly happen when one hasn't figured out how to accept and let go of their unpleasant feelings.

Children may benefit from this by having their internal experiences respected, accepted, and understood. We can also sometimes provide them with pertinent knowledge without necessarily addressing their problems or hastening the resolution of their emotional outbursts. Additionally, we may "hold the space" for them while validating their feelings, allowing them to completely express those feelings and, if required, come up with solutions.

Allowing kids to experience things
To help youngsters learn to persist, we must let them encounter difficulty without interfering or responding. Sometimes it might be more

beneficial for a youngster to struggle and even fail with a task or circumstance rather than succeed with help.

Children may develop a constructive attitude about failure, learn to accept it, and think about making adjustments for the better in their own lives. By simply providing them with the knowledge they need and, if required, validating their feelings, we can assist them if they are irritated or experiencing another strong emotion.

We naturally want to support our kids as parents, and we often do it without even realizing it. By sparing children from failure or difficulty, we can mistakenly believe that we are boosting their self-esteem or imparting knowledge, but in reality, the reverse may happen. By intervening when they are having difficulty, we reduce their tenacity and, when we rescue them from failure, we increase their discomfort with failure.

A youngster who does not feel comfortable failing or going through difficulty will develop dependency and dread, which will lower their level of confidence overall. Additionally, a common error is to attempt to address a kid's issue before waiting for them to be in a receptive condition. This simply causes the youngster to become more unhappy, defensive, and close off. Before we can expect children to be open enough to solve problems or make good decisions, we must first connect with, affirm, and allow for their whole emotional experience.

However, inevitably, we will sometimes save children from hardship or failure; we shouldn't feel bad about it. As long as it isn't given too often and we make it clear that we believe in their inherent skills, lending a helping hand is a fantastic way to assist a youngster who asks for it and appreciates it.

Validation

"Validation" refers to non-judgmental acknowledgment and communication of knowledge of the causes of another person's feelings. Without dramatizing, victimizing, or presuming the child's genuine emotional condition, we may do this with children in a matter-of-fact manner and with a friendly tone while naming events and the child's internal view.

Although it is not our responsibility to "fix" their feelings, we may support them through this process of straightforward affirmation or acknowledgment. Getting too engaged in or untrusting their emotional process might make them feel more stressed. We may also consider what they could be attempting to express or heal, and if required, we can assist them in doing so.

For our kids to feel seen, understood, and accepted while they are experiencing strong emotions, we may adopt the technique of validation. This will enable them to feel the same way about themselves. Children who feel validated are more likely to digest experiences, pick viewpoints and responses that are more positive and realistic, and become emotionally resilient. This alone fosters empowerment and self-assurance.

Children learn that feelings are not terrifying or unpleasant, but rather a natural aspect of human experience through being accepted, connected to, given simple words to aid in processing, and supported when experiencing strong emotions. They will eventually realize for themselves that such routine occurrences aren't such a huge problem, get beyond strong emotions, and develop their answers. They get through this process more quickly and successfully when they feel validated.

This method strengthens the bond and trust between parents and children, which is necessary for a solid foundation of felt security. And that promotes resilience and self-worth.

How Do We Negate and How Can We Stop It?
There are many ways that parents unintentionally undermine rather than validate their children's emotions, including denial of an actual issue, avoidance of the child or their words or behaviors while they are reacting, distraction from the reaction, and instilling fear (by means such as threatening, punishing, or communicating that the child is undeserving of

acceptance while reacting by saying things like, "I will talk to you when you are being 'nice'").

These parenting practices have less to do with the kid and more to do with the parent and either the wrong signals they have gotten about how to manage children's emotions, their own experience as children, or their troubles with emotions (often owing to their childhood experience). Because of the views they experienced as children from adults who did not understand or respect the significance and functioning of emotions, many people today find emotions unpleasant. Fortunately, when it comes to emotions, we now comprehend them far better.

The adoption of maladaptive psychological defense mechanisms in children is associated with having such responses to our children's emotions as those previously indicated, which prevents the development of emotional intelligence, maturity, and resilience. This has been demonstrated to result in undesirable responses to social pressures and life's stresses as well as making one more susceptible to sickness.

We can view this as an opportunity to address our emotional healing as well as a sign of something we can work on to help our children develop resilience, emotional empowerment, and intelligence when we observe ourselves reacting in ways like denial, avoidance, distraction, "fixing," or inducing fear while our children are experiencing strong emotions, which most of us will do to some extent. When our baggage gets in the way, we are unable to be present for what is going on with our kids. Realizing that this is a situation that we can fix rather than one that our children are creating and is beyond our control might feel more empowered.

One of the best indicators of both resiliency and success may be emotional intelligence. When we concentrate on constructive emotional reactions, it helps. Even though it doesn't always feel like it at the moment that it becomes clear, I think this window into our emotional responses is one of parenthood's greatest gifts.

Keeping Silence

Making a secure and supportive emotional and physical environment for someone to process whatever is going on in their life is known as "holding space" for them. We may connect with children nonverbally by lowering ourselves to their level and giving them a loving smile, embrace, or a comforting pat on the back while they feel strong emotions. In a secure environment, this enables people to accept, completely express, and let go of their feelings.

Additionally, connection causes the neural system of a kid to generate hormones that reduce stress. These hormones aid in problem-solving and provide children with the experience-based confidence they need to be resilient in the face of a variety of obstacles. It's also crucial to express to the youngster in the heat of the moment that they are just experiencing an emotion, that they are not that emotion right now, and that it will pass. This may seem like a straightforward idea to adults, but a youngster may not be aware of this since the feeling might seem so overwhelming and frightening to them.

Children learn that emotions, hardship, and failure are not a huge thing when we encourage their emotional intelligence by recognizing the importance of emotional expression, letting them have their experiences, validating their feelings, and holding the space for them to express their emotions. On their terms, when they are prepared, individuals may learn to accept and then let go of the urge to have a strong response.

Chapter Eight

Practicing Emotional Intelligence through Play and Activities

The development of critical emotional abilities in children may be accelerated and made more fun by having them practice emotional intelligence via play and other activities. With the help of play-based learning, children may discover their emotions, comprehend those of others, and develop good emotion management skills in a fun and secure setting. Children may build a solid foundation for their emotional health and social connections by incorporating emotional intelligence into play and activities. Here are some games and activities you may use to improve emotional intelligence:

Play activities that are centered on emotions to get youngsters thinking about and expressing their emotions. For instance, children can act out various emotions while trying to predict which emotion is being depicted. The ability to convey one's emotions is improved through this game.

Children may acquire crucial emotional abilities in a fun and interesting way by introducing emotional intelligence into play and activities. Children are better able to handle their emotions in real-life circumstances as they get experience detecting, comprehending, and controlling their emotions via play. The foundation for developing emotional intelligence and raising an emotionally aware and empathic generation is laid by these fun encounters.

Emotional Intelligence Activities for Kids

Children may take turns playing out various emotions silently while others try to determine which one is being depicted. After each round, talk about the emotions you had and how they related to actual circumstances.

Make bingo cards featuring a range of emotions for "emotion bingo." Encourage kids to share personal stories about each emotion as they recognize and name them during the game, fostering emotional expressiveness.

Kids may maintain a feelings notebook in which they can record their everyday emotions via writing or drawing. Encourage them to examine their emotions and talk about any trends or changes they observe over time.

Give children magazines and art materials so they may make a collage depicting their feelings. Inquire about the inspiration for their collage and the feelings they decided to depict.

Children should practice producing various facial expressions in front of a mirror to help them recognize and comprehend the many emotions they can encounter.

Create cards with images of different emotional expressions and instruct children to arrange them into positive, negative, and neutral categories while explaining the reasoning behind their decisions.

Set up stations expressing various emotions using images or objects throughout the space. Children may round the room and point out the emotions at each station before explaining their choice.

Design a board game where children play out various situations and react to difficulties experienced by the characters with empathy and understanding.

Children may role-play situations in which they must deal with emotions and disagreements while coming to a cooperatively satisfying conclusion.

Some kids sit in a circle and alternately share something for which they are thankful while also talking about the pleasant feelings that come with appreciation.

Guide children through mindful breathing techniques to help them connect with their emotions and react calmly to stressful circumstances.

Storytelling with Emotions: Work together to write tales in which children add emotional undertones to the characters' experiences and talk about the emotions that drive them.

Use weather metaphors to depict emotions, such as sunny for cheerfulness and stormy for anger. Children may alternate roles as "weather reporters" and provide their daily emotional forecasts.

Arrange an "empathy walk" where children may act out various characters experiencing various emotions. They may communicate their emotions, and others can practice understanding and empathetic responses.

Give children art tools so they may make paintings that are based on emotions, using various colors and brushstrokes to symbolize various emotions.

Make sculptures that convey emotions, and use clay or play dough. Children may talk about the feelings that inspired their works.

Practice positive affirmations as a group, paying particular attention to boosting self-assurance and encouraging self-awareness.

Blindfold one kid and ask the others to express various emotions in words or pictures for the blindfolded youngster to identify.

A mindful nature walk may help youngsters connect with nature by encouraging them to notice and talk about their emotions.

Make emotional-themed puzzles and ask children to identify the emotions they refer to.

Give children puzzles with emotion terms to complete while you talk to them about the correlations and definitions of each emotion.

Play music, and when it ends, youngsters dance or make expressions on their faces to convey the emotion they are feeling.

Create an emotion face flipbook with illustrations so that children may flip through it and talk about the feelings they perceive.

Sit in a circle, and have each kid describe a feeling they had that day. People might react empathetically or express comparable feelings.

Chapter Nine

Conclusion

We consider the transformational path we've taken to equip our kids with critical emotional skills. We have examined the breadth of emotional intelligence and its significant influence on children's lives throughout this book. We now know that emotional intelligence is a dynamic talent that can be developed and nourished with deliberate direction and assistance.

We've learned from the pages of this book that emotional awareness and expression are the foundation of emotional intelligence. Children can manage emotions with confidence and authenticity when we provide an open and accepting atmosphere where they feel secure to express their feelings. We are aware of the enormous influence empathy and compassion have on developing deep relationships with people and promoting a culture of kindness.

We've also looked at how emotional intelligence gives kids the crucial abilities of emotional control and resilience. Now that they have the skills to do so, our kids will be able to handle their emotions well and overcome obstacles in life with unflinching courage. They adopt a growth mentality that encourages learning from errors, paving the way for continuous improvement and personal progress.

As parents, educators, and other caregivers, we've learned to promote kids' social and communication skills, giving them the confidence to handle interpersonal interactions with assertiveness, empathy, and understanding. We've accepted our responsibilities as emotional mentors, prepared with specialist knowledge and doable tactics to support kids' emotional and social development.

Our children's interest has been sparked by play-based learning and activities, as they delightfully explore and expressively express their feelings. We have accepted the beauty of mindfulness and the potential it has to support kids in connecting with their feelings and handling obstacles in life in a calm and collected manner.

Let's bring the essence of emotional intelligence into our homes, schools, and communities as we wrap up this book. Let's teach our kids the emotional skills they need to face life's challenges with fortitude and grace by serving as examples of empathy, understanding, and compassion.

May our kids develop into emotionally astute adults who lead with compassion, understanding, and empathy and pave the way for the world to change for the better. And may this book serve as a regular reminder that developing emotional intelligence is a lifetime path of personal progress.

As we create a future full of emotionally intelligent, powerful, and compassionate people who elevate and inspire others around them, let's embrace the core of emotional intelligence in children.